MOTIVATIONAL QUOTES FOR
SUCCESS

summersdale

MOTIVATIONAL QUOTES FOR SUCCESS

An Hachette UK Company
www.hachette.co.uk

Summersdale Publishers Ltd
Part of Octopus Publishing Group Limited
Carmelite House
50 Victoria Embankment
LONDON
EC4Y 0DZ
UK

www.summersdale.com

Printed and bound in China

ISBN: 978-1-78685-965-5

Substantial discounts on bulk quantities of Summersdale books are available to corporations, professional associations and other organizations. For details contact general enquiries: telephone: +44 (0) 1243 771107 or email: enquiries@summersdale.com.

To...............................

From...........................

YOU CAN'T
PUT A LIMIT
ON ANYTHING.
THE MORE
YOU DREAM,
THE FARTHER
YOU GET.

MICHAEL PHELPS

Surround yourself **only** with people who are going to take you **higher**.

Oprah Winfrey

GIVE US THE TOOLS AND WE WILL FINISH THE JOB.

WINSTON CHURCHILL

THE FORMULA OF
HAPPINESS AND
SUCCESS IS JUST BEING
ACTUALLY YOURSELF,
IN THE MOST VIVID
POSSIBLE WAY
YOU CAN.

Meryl Streep

Obstacles are those frightful things you see when you take your eyes off your goal.

Henry Ford

ACHIEVEMENT IS TALENT PLUS PREPARATION.

Malcolm Gladwell

Run when you can,
walk if you have to,
crawl if you must;
just never give up.

Dean Karnazes

"

ALL OUR DREAMS
CAN COME TRUE, IF WE
HAVE THE COURAGE
TO PURSUE THEM.

Walt Disney

"

66

THE MISTAKE IS
TO IMAGINE THAT
PERFECTION IS POSSIBLE
WHEN THE VERY IDEA
IS UNTHINKABLE.

Luis Figo

TRY AND FAIL, BUT NEVER FAIL TO TRY.

JARED LETO

There is **almost** no such thing as ready. There is **only now**.

Hugh Laurie

THINGS DO NOT HAPPEN. THINGS ARE MADE TO HAPPEN.

JOHN F. KENNEDY

"

THANKFULLY, PERSISTENCE IS A GREAT SUBSTITUTE FOR TALENT.

STEVE MARTIN

What is important is to believe in something so strongly that you're never discouraged.

SALMA HAYEK

I am thankful to all
those who said no.
It's because of them
I did it myself.

Wayne W. Dyer

"

JUST REMEMBER, YOU
CAN DO ANYTHING
YOU SET YOUR MIND TO,
BUT IT TAKES ACTION,
PERSEVERANCE, AND
FACING YOUR FEARS.

Gillian Anderson

I don't measure a man's **success** by how high he **climbs** but how high he **bounces** when he hits bottom.

George S. Patton

IT'S HARD WORK
THAT MAKES
THINGS HAPPEN.
IT'S HARD WORK
THAT CREATES
CHANGE.

Shonda Rhimes

THE BIGGEST RISK
IS NOT TAKING
ANY RISK.

MARK ZUCKERBERG

66

THE DICTIONARY IS THE
ONLY PLACE WHERE
SUCCESS COMES
BEFORE WORK.

Vince Lombardi

99

" BEING REALISTIC IS THE MOST COMMONLY TRAVELLED ROAD TO MEDIOCRITY.

Will Smith

"

BIG SHOTS ARE ONLY LITTLE SHOTS WHO KEEP SHOOTING.

Christopher Morley

I MAY NOT BE
THERE YET, BUT
I'M CLOSER
THAN I WAS
YESTERDAY.

ANONYMOUS

Perseverance is the hard work you do after you get tired of doing the hard work you already did.

NEWT GINGRICH

You can often
change your
circumstances
by changing
your attitude.

Eleanor Roosevelt

Nobody has enough **talent** to live on talent alone. Even when you have talent, a life without **work** goes nowhere.

Arsène Wenger

"

THE REALITY IS:
SOMETIMES YOU LOSE.
AND YOU'RE NEVER
TOO GOOD TO LOSE.
YOU'RE NEVER TOO
BIG TO LOSE.

Beyoncé

"

Success and failure.
We think of them as
opposites, but they're
really not. They're
companions – the hero
and the sidekick.

LAURENCE SHAMES

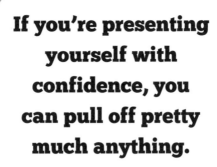

If you're presenting yourself with confidence, you can pull off pretty much anything.

Katy Perry

IF YOU'RE WALKING
DOWN THE RIGHT PATH
AND YOU'RE WILLING
TO KEEP WALKING,
EVENTUALLY YOU'LL
MAKE PROGRESS.

Barack Obama

WHO SEEKS
SHALL FIND.

SOPHOCLES

Ignore the naysayers. Really the only option is head down and focus on the job.

Chris Pine

If at first you don't **succeed**, you're running about **average**.

M. H. Alderson

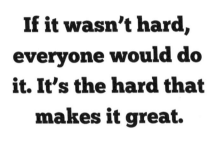

If it wasn't hard, everyone would do it. It's the hard that makes it great.

Tom Hanks

There is no point at which you can say, "Well, I'm successful now. I might as well take a nap."

CARRIE FISHER

"

THOSE WHO DARE TO FAIL MISERABLY CAN ACHIEVE GREATLY.

JOHN F. KENNEDY

"

"

IF YOU CAN DO WHAT
YOU DO BEST AND BE
HAPPY, YOU'RE FURTHER
ALONG IN LIFE THAN
MOST PEOPLE.

Leonardo DiCaprio

"

ROCK BOTTOM BECAME THE SOLID FOUNDATION ON WHICH I REBUILT MY LIFE.

J. K. Rowling

"

FLAMING ENTHUSIASM,
BACKED UP BY HORSE
SENSE AND PERSISTENCE,
IS THE QUALITY THAT
MOST FREQUENTLY
MAKES FOR SUCCESS.

Dale Carnegie

"

OPPORTUNITIES MULTIPLY AS THEY ARE SEIZED.

Sun Tzu

I didn't get there by **wishing** for it or hoping for it, but by **working** for it.

Estée Lauder

DON'T BE AFRAID.
BE FOCUSED.
BE DETERMINED.
BE HOPEFUL.
BE EMPOWERED.

Michelle Obama

YESTERDAY'S HOME RUNS DON'T WIN TODAY'S GAMES.

BABE RUTH

THE WORK THAT I'M PROUDEST OF IS THE WORK THAT I'M MOST AFRAID OF.

STEVEN SPIELBERG

66

BE SO GOOD THEY
CAN'T IGNORE YOU.

Steve Martin

You keep putting one foot in front of the other, and then one day you look back and you've climbed a mountain.

TOM HIDDLESTON

When you become comfortable with uncertainty, infinite possibilities open up in your life.

Eckhart Tolle

DON'T LET ANYONE TELL YOU WHAT YOU CAN AND CAN'T DO OR ACHIEVE. DO WHAT YOU WANT TO DO AND BE WHO YOU WANT TO BE.

Emma Watson

Ultimately, there's one investment that supersedes all others: invest in yourself.

Warren Buffett

Just as **iron** sharpens iron, positive people will inspire you to be **positive**.

Rihanna

DONE IS BETTER THAN PERFECT.

SHERYL SANDBERG

You can't determine where you start in life, but you can determine where you end up.

KARREN BRADY

IT'S IMPORTANT TO
ACKNOWLEDGE THE
MISTAKES YOU'VE
MADE IN LIFE, BECAUSE
IT'S REALLY THROUGH
THOSE THAT YOU
LEARN THINGS.

Andrew Lloyd Webber

YOU ARE NEVER
TOO OLD TO SET
ANOTHER GOAL
OR TO DREAM A
NEW DREAM.

LES BROWN

I'm one of the least competitive people you'll ever meet. Except with myself.

Daniel Craig

SOMEDAY IS NOT A DAY OF THE WEEK.

Janet Dailey

HARD WORK BEATS TALENT WHEN TALENT DOESN'T WORK HARD.

Tim Notke

Challenges are
what make life
interesting
and overcoming them
is what makes life
meaningful.

Joshua J. Marine

Perseverance is not a long race; it is many short races one after the other.

Walter Elliot

Today I will do what others won't, so tomorrow I can accomplish what others can't.

JERRY RICE

Aim for the sky and you'll reach the ceiling. Aim for the ceiling and you'll stay on the floor.

Bill Shankly

Through **perseverance**
many people win
success out of what
seemed destined to be
certain failure.

Benjamin Disraeli

SOMEONE ELSE'S SUCCESS IS NOT YOUR FAILURE.

Jim Parsons

CHALLENGE YOURSELF; IT'S THE ONLY PATH WHICH LEADS TO GROWTH.

MORGAN FREEMAN

" —

NOTHING WILL SERVE
YOU BETTER THAN
A STRONG WORK
ETHIC. NOTHING.

Robert Downey Jr

YOU MAY ENCOUNTER MANY DEFEATS, BUT YOU MUST NOT BE DEFEATED.

MAYA ANGELOU

WHEN YOU'RE USED TO
BEING PREPARED TO
REJECT CONVENTIONAL
WISDOM, IT LEAVES YOU
OPEN TO LEARN MORE.

Mayim Bialik

FAILURE IS SIMPLY THE OPPORTUNITY TO BEGIN AGAIN, THIS TIME MORE INTELLIGENTLY.

Henry Ford

Follow your passions, follow your heart, and the things you need will come.

Elizabeth Taylor

WHEREVER YOU ARE –
BE ALL THERE.

Jim Elliot

Life's problems wouldn't be called "hurdles" if there wasn't a way to get over them.

ANONYMOUS

NOTHING IS IMPOSSIBLE, THE WORD ITSELF SAYS "I'M POSSIBLE"!

AUDREY HEPBURN

**Open your heart
to the sky. Live.**

Adam Gnade

You've achieved **success** in your field when you **don't know** whether what you're doing is work or play.

Warren Beatty

THE SHELL MUST BREAK BEFORE THE BIRD CAN FLY.

ALFRED TENNYSON

You have to just dive over the edge. You haven't got time to mess about.

RALPH FIENNES

FAILURE IS SUCCESS IF WE LEARN FROM IT.

Malcolm Forbes

DON'T FIND FAULT, FIND A REMEDY.

TONY ROBBINS

IF YOU DO NOT
HAVE COURAGE,
YOU MAY NOT HAVE
THE OPPORTUNITY TO
USE ANY OF YOUR
OTHER VIRTUES.

Samuel L. Jackson

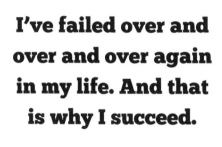

"

LIFE IS TOO FRAGILE
AND VALUABLE TO
BE SPENT DOING
SOMETHING YOU HATE.

Duncan Bannatyne

BELIEVE YOU CAN AND YOU'RE HALFWAY THERE.

THEODORE ROOSEVELT

There is no reason not to be **motivated**. You cannot always be the **best**. But you can do your best.

Sebastian Vettel

66

IF YOU ASK ME WHAT
I CAME TO DO IN THIS
WORLD... I WILL ANSWER
YOU: I AM HERE TO
LIVE OUT LOUD.

Émile Zola

Most things don't work out as expected, but what happens instead often turns out to be the good stuff.

JUDI DENCH

THE GOAL ISN'T TO LIVE FOREVER, THE GOAL IS TO CREATE SOMETHING THAT WILL.

Chuck Palahniuk

WHENEVER YOU FALL, PICK SOMETHING UP.

OSWALD AVERY

THERE IS ONLY ONE
THING THAT MAKES
A DREAM IMPOSSIBLE
TO ACHIEVE: THE
FEAR OF FAILURE.

Paulo Coelho

Tell me, what is it you plan to do with your one wild and precious life?

Mary Oliver

"

AS HUMAN BEINGS
WE HAVE UNLIMITED
POTENTIAL AND
IMAGINATION.

Deepak Chopra

"

If you put out **150 per cent,** then you can always expect **100 per cent** back.

Justin Timberlake

66

FOLLOW YOUR DREAMS,
BECAUSE YOUR DREAMS
WON'T FOLLOW YOU.

Amanda Holden

Be humble, hungry and always be the hardest worker in the room.

DWAYNE JOHNSON

IF EVERYTHING WAS
PERFECT, YOU WOULD
NEVER LEARN AND YOU
WOULD NEVER GROW.

Beyoncé

"

FIND SOMEBODY
TO BE SUCCESSFUL
FOR. RAISE THEIR
HOPES. THINK OF
THEIR NEEDS.

Barack Obama

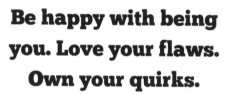

Be happy with being you. Love your flaws. Own your quirks.

Ariana Grande

There is no passion in playing small – in settling for a life less than you are capable of living.

NELSON MANDELA

NEVER GIVE UP, FOR THAT'S JUST THE PLACE AND TIME THAT THE TIDE'LL TURN.

Harriet Beecher Stowe

YOU ONLY GET TO BE
GOOD BY MAKING
MISTAKES, AND YOU
ONLY GET TO BE REAL BY
BEING IMPERFECT.

Julianne Moore

EXPECT PROBLEMS AND EAT THEM FOR BREAKFAST.

ALFRED A. MONTAPERT

**FALL SEVEN TIMES,
STAND UP EIGHT.**

Japanese proverb

With **ordinary** talent and **extraordinary** perseverance, all things are attainable.

Thomas Fowell Buxton

YOU MISS 100 PER CENT OF THE SHOTS YOU DON'T TAKE.

WAYNE GRETZKY

THE ROAD TO SUCCESS IS ALWAYS UNDER CONSTRUCTION.

Lily Tomlin

Don't worry about being successful but work toward being significant and the success will naturally follow.

OPRAH WINFREY

Follow your dreams and don't let anyone stop you. Never say never.

Justin Bieber

SUCCESS SEEMS TO BE
LARGELY A MATTER OF
HANGING ON AFTER
OTHERS HAVE LET GO.

William Feather

NEVER LET THE FEAR OF STRIKING OUT KEEP YOU FROM PLAYING THE GAME.

Babe Ruth

YOU CAN WASTE YOUR LIFE DRAWING LINES, OR YOU CAN LIVE YOUR LIFE CROSSING THEM.

Shonda Rhimes

Develop success from **failures**. Discouragement and failure are two of the **surest** stepping stones to success.

Dale Carnegie

KEEP YOUR EYES ON THE FINISH LINE AND NOT ON THE TURMOIL AROUND YOU.

Rihanna

THE ONLY FAILURE IS NOT TO TRY.

GEORGE CLOONEY

Success will never be
a big step in the future,
success is a small step
taken just now.

JONATAN MÅRTENSSON

"

WORK LIKE THERE
IS SOMEONE ELSE
WORKING 24 HOURS
A DAY TO TAKE IT
AWAY FROM YOU.

Mark Cuban

I WOULD RATHER
LIVE AND DIE BY
MY OWN HAND. IF
MY STUFF SUCKS,
AT LEAST I MADE
IT SUCK.

ZENDAYA

THERE ARE ALWAYS
THINGS YOU CAN
LEARN, EVERY
SINGLE DAY. THERE IS
ALWAYS SPACE FOR
IMPROVEMENT.

Lewis Hamilton

THE FIRST STEP IS YOU HAVE TO SAY THAT YOU CAN.

WILL SMITH

All good ideas start out as bad ideas, that's why it takes so long.

Steven Spielberg

I COULDN'T WAIT FOR SUCCESS, SO I WENT AHEAD WITHOUT IT.

JONATHAN WINTERS

Fortune does favour the **bold** and you'll never know what you're **capable** of if you don't try.

Sheryl Sandberg

**Action is the
foundational key
to all success.**

Pablo Picasso

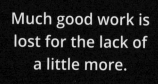

Much good work is
lost for the lack of
a little more.

EDWARD H. HARRIMAN

ALL LIFE IS AN
EXPERIMENT. THE MORE
EXPERIMENTS YOU
MAKE THE BETTER.

Ralph Waldo Emerson

When life puts you in tough situations, don't say "why me", say "try me".

Anonymous

SUCCESS IS
99 PER CENT
FAILURE.

Soichiro Honda

Only those who will **risk** going too far can possibly find out **how far** one can go.

T. S. Eliot

No one knows what he can do until he tries.

Publilius Syrus

THERE ARE NO MISTAKES, ONLY OPPORTUNITIES.

Tina Fey

When obstacles arise,
you change your direction
to reach your goal, you
do not change your
decision to get there.

ZIG ZIGLAR

SET YOUR GOALS HIGH AND DON'T STOP TILL YOU GET THERE.

BO JACKSON

WORKING HARD
FOR SOMETHING WE
DON'T CARE ABOUT
IS CALLED STRESS;
WORKING HARD FOR
SOMETHING WE LOVE
IS CALLED PASSION.

Simon Sinek

WHEN YOU GO THROUGH HARDSHIPS AND DECIDE NOT TO SURRENDER, THAT IS STRENGTH.

Arnold Schwarzenegger

You never know if **anything** is going to work. You just **throw yourself** into it and do your best.

Steve Carell

I really don't think life is about the "I-could-have-beens". Life is only about the "I-tried-to-do".

NIKKI GIOVANNI

Don't think
about your errors
or failures,
otherwise you'll
never do a thing.

Bill Murray

LIFE IS VERY
INTERESTING... IN
THE END, SOME OF
YOUR GREATEST
PAINS BECOME YOUR
GREATEST STRENGTHS.

Drew Barrymore

Believe in yourself, take on your challenges, dig deep within yourself to conquer fears.

Chantal Sutherland

HARD WORK WILL ALWAYS BRING OPPORTUNITIES.

KARREN BRADY

NOTHING WILL STOP
YOU BEING CREATIVE
MORE EFFECTIVELY
AS THE FEAR OF
MAKING A MISTAKE.

John Cleese

Many of life's **failures** are people who did not realise **how close** they were to success when they gave up.

Thomas A. Edison

I ATTRIBUTE MY SUCCESS TO THIS: I NEVER GAVE OR TOOK AN EXCUSE.

FLORENCE NIGHTINGALE

It's always too
early to quit.

Norman Vincent Peale

OPPORTUNITIES DON'T HAPPEN. YOU CREATE THEM.

Chris Grosser

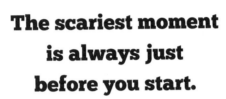

The scariest moment
is always just
before you start.

Stephen King

Practice isn't the thing you do once you're good. It's the thing you do that makes you good.

MALCOLM GLADWELL

I CAN,
THEREFORE I AM.

Simone Weil

SOMETIMES YOU CAN
HAVE THE SMALLEST
ROLE IN THE SMALLEST
PRODUCTION AND STILL
HAVE A BIG IMPACT.

Neil Patrick Harris

There is no magic
to achievement.
It's really about
hard work, choices
and persistence.

Michelle Obama

Some people dream of success... while others wake up and work hard at it.

Anonymous

TO KNOW ONESELF,
ONE MUST ASSERT
ONESELF.

Albert Camus

WITH DRIVE AND A BIT OF TALENT, YOU CAN MOVE MOUNTAINS.

DWAYNE JOHNSON

I CAME, I SAW, I CONQUERED.

Julius Caesar

Put blinders onto those things that conspire to hold you back, especially the ones in your own head.

MERYL STREEP

YOU DON'T HAVE TO BE PERFECT TO ACHIEVE YOUR DREAMS.

KATY PERRY

"

OUR GREATEST GLORY IS
NOT IN NEVER FALLING,
BUT IN RISING EVERY
TIME WE FALL.

Confucius

"

If you're interested in finding out more about our books, find us on Facebook at **Summersdale Publishers** and follow us on Twitter at **@Summersdale**.

www.summersdale.com